Windows 10

Withdrawn

Fast Start

A Quick Start Guide to Windows 10

Smart Brain Training Solutions

Thank you for purchasing *Windows 10 Fast Start*! We hope you'll look for other *Fast Start* guides from Smart Brain Training Solutions.

Books by Smart Brain Training Solutions, written by William R. Stanek and based on his full-length Personal Trainers, contain the fast, focused information you need to get up and running with new technologies.

Cover Design: Creative Designs Ltd.
Editorial Development: Andover Publishing Solutions
Technical Review: L & L Technical Content Services

You can provide feedback related to this book by emailing the author at williamstanek@aol.com. Please use the name of the book as the subject line.

Version: 1.0.2

> **Note** I may periodically update this text and the version number shown above will let you know which version you are working with. If there's a specific feature you'd like me to write about in an update, message me on Facebook (http://facebook.com/williamstanekauthor). Please keep in mind readership of this book determines how much time I can dedicate to it.

Table of Contents

1. Kicking the Tires

Ready to kick the tires and get to know Windows 10? Windows 10 isn't legacy Windows. It has an all new look and an interface that has some features of Windows 7, some features of Windows 8 and many new options. So much has changed, in fact, that from login to logout, you'll be required to work in new ways to get tasks done.

Windows 10 runs on tablets, desktops, laptops, smartphones and other types of computing devices. Rather than mentioning all of these types of devices each time I talk about the operating system, I'll simply say your computer, your device or I may refer to your Windows 10 device. When I do this, I'm talking about all of the various types of devices Windows 10 runs on.

Using Touchscreens

Windows 10 supports two primary input types:

- Keyboard and mouse
- Touchscreen

While the keyboard and mouse are standard, a touchscreen allows you to manipulate on-screen elements in new ways. You can:

- **Tap**   Touch an on-screen element with your finger. A tap or double-tap of elements on the screen generally is the equivalent of a mouse click or double-click.
- **Press and hold**   Press your finger down on an on-screen element and leave it there for a few seconds. Pressing and holding elements on the screen generally is the equivalent of a right-click.

- **Pan (slide to scroll)** Touch and drag across the screen with one or two fingers. Panning shows another part of a window that has scroll bars. Also referred to as sliding to scroll.
- **Pinch** Touch an item with two or more fingers and then move the fingers toward each other. Pinching shows less information.
- **Rotate** Touch two points on the screen and then twist. Rotating turns an item on screen in a clockwise or counter-clockwise direction.
- **Slide in from edge** Starting from the edge of the screen, slide across the screen without lifting your finger. Sliding in from the left edge shows open apps and allows you to switch between them easily. Sliding in from the top or bottom edge shows commands for the active element.
- **Stretch** Touch an item with two or more fingers and then move the fingers away from each other. Stretching shows more information.
- **Swipe to select** Slide an item a short distance in the opposite direction compared to how the page scrolls. Swiping in this way selects the item and also may bring up related commands. If press and hold doesn't display commands and options for an item, try using swipe to select instead.

Keep in mind that throughout this guide, where I have used click, right-click and double-click, you can also use touch equivalents, tap, press and hold, and double tap. Also, when your Windows 10 device doesn't have a physical keyboard, you are able to enter text by using the onscreen keyboard. If a device has no physical keyboard, simply touch an input area on the screen, such as the Search box, to display the onscreen keyboard.

Getting Signed In

Windows 10 has a new sign-in process that works with touchscreens as well as a keyboard and mouse. When you start or wake Windows 10, you'll see a preview screen. With a touch screen, swipe up to reveal the login screen. With a keyboard and mouse, simply press a key on the keyboard or click a mouse button to reveal the login screen.

By default, login is always required when you start or wake your Windows 10 device. The way login works depends on whether your computer is part of a business network. For computers that aren't joined to a business network, you have many login options, including:

- **Password**   A password is a mix of upper and lowercase letters, numbers and special characters, usually 8 or more characters in length. To login with a password, click your user name on the login screen, type your password and then press Enter on the keyboard or click the sign-in button (which shows a right-facing arrow).
- **Pin**   A pin is a sequence of 4 or more numbers. To login with a pin, click your user name on the login screen, type your pin and then press Enter on the keyboard or click the sign-in button (which shows a right-facing arrow).
- **Picture password**   A picture password is a unique series of movements on a previously-selected photo, such as a line drawn between two flowers and a circle drawn around a specific flower. To login with a picture password, click your user name on the login screen and then use the touch interface to make the required movements.

> **Tip**   If you're having trouble logging in using a password or pin, click the reveal icon (which has a symbol representing an eye) to display the exact text you typed.

User name and password are the default login technique. You can add a pin, picture password or both using Settings. Settings has replaced Control Panel as the go to resource for most configuration options.

In business networks, the domain settings control whether you can use pins and picture passwords. In a domain, if your user name isn't displayed on the login screen, click Other User, type your user name, type your password and then press Enter on the keyboard or click the sign-in button.

Entering and Exiting Tablet Mode

When you're using Windows 10 on a tablet PC, tablet mode usually is what you want to use. However, tablet mode changes the way Windows works and you may either love or hate it.

In tablet mode, the Start Menu is replaced with a Start screen, as shown in Figure 1. The standard Start screen options include:

- **Options button** Shown in the upper left corner, you must click this button to display the Start options panel (or when working with Start, by swiping in from the left).
- **Power button** Provides access to power options, which can include: sleep, shutdown and restart.
- **Apps button** Displays the All Apps list, which you can use to start programs not shown on the Start screen.
- **Start button** Switches between Start and the desktop.

Figure 1 Accessing Start in tablet mode.

When you click an app on Start, the app opens on the desktop in full-screen mode. The Task View button provides one way to switch between apps. Click the Task View button to see a preview of open apps and then click the app you want to open.

In Tablet mode, app icons on the taskbar are hidden by default. This means you won't see any items pinned to the taskbar or icons for open windows or running apps.

All of these snap behaviors are configurable and controlled with System Settings by following these steps:

1. Click Start and then click Settings.
2. In the Settings dialog box, click System. On the System page, click Tablet Mode.
3. In the main pane, use these options to manage the way tablet mode works:

- If you don't want to use tablet mode, you can disable the feature by toggling the Make Windows More Touch-Friendly... option to the Off position.
- If you want Windows 10 to go to the desktop instead of Start when you login, set When I Sign In to Go To The Desktop.
- If you want access to pinned items, open windows and running apps via the taskbar, you can disable by setting Hide App Icons... to the Off position by clicking it.

> **Tip** Not used to toggle switches? Toggles have On/Off positions. You change the position from On to Off or Off to On simply by clicking the toggle.

2. Navigating the Accounts Maze

Windows 10 supports:

* Local accounts
* Domain accounts

The account types available depend on whether your computer is part of a business network. If your computer isn't part of a business network, your computer has only local accounts. As the designator implies, local accounts are created on your computer. Otherwise, if your computer is part of a business network, your computer has both local accounts and domain accounts.

> **Real World**   Domain accounts exist on the business network, as part of either an Active Directory domain or an Azure-based Active Directory domain. The difference between the two has to do with whether your organization hosts its own servers. If your organization hosts its own servers, you connect to a business network that is part of a standard Active Directory domain. If your organization doesn't host its own servers, you connect to a business network that is serviced via Internet-hosted servers that are part of an Azure AD domain.

Local and Domain Accounts

Local accounts and domain accounts can be Internet-connected to sync settings, documents and purchases across devices. Two types of Internet-connected accounts are supported:

* Microsoft accounts
* School or work accounts

You can connect Microsoft accounts and school or work accounts to both local and domain accounts to get the Internet-connected benefits of syncing settings, documents, purchases and more. With a non-business computer or device, you simply use the Microsoft account for first sign in to create a local account that uses Microsoft account for login. You also can add accounts using the Microsoft account information to create additional local accounts that use Microsoft accounts for login. From then on, the local accounts and the Microsoft accounts are synced and you login using the Microsoft account.

With a non-business computer or device, you can add a school or work account as well to get the get the Internet-connected benefits of syncing settings, documents and more with Office 365 or other Microsoft business services. Here, you use Settings to connect to the account. Thereafter, whenever you login with your local account or Microsoft account, you receive the additional connected benefits of the business service.

> **Note**   Determining whether you are using a local account or a Microsoft account is easy. Local accounts use a name string, such as TedG or SaraH. Microsoft accounts use email addresses, such as williams@imaginedlands.com.

Accessing Business Networks

When your computer is part of a business network, you can login using a local account or a domain account, either of which can be connected to a Microsoft account, a school or work account or both. As before, when you connect a local account to a Microsoft account, settings, documents, purchases and more are synced across devices. When you add a school or work account to a local account or a Microsoft account, the accounts similarly become connected and synced.

When you connect a Microsoft account or a school or work account to a domain account, the accounts are synced but you continue to login using the domain account. Switching between local accounts and domain accounts requires using the Other Account option on the login screen.

On the Other Accounts screen, you specify the account name to use in *Node\name* format where *Node* is the location for login and *name* is the user name. The Node can be a domain name, the name of the device, or "." which refers to the local device. For example, if you want to log in to the ImaginedLands domain as WilliamS, you'd specify the account name as imaginedlands\williams. If the local device is named Computer14 and you want to log in as TedG, you can specify the account name as either Computer14\TedG or .\TedG.

3. Making the Most of Your Desktop Space

No, that's not a typo in the heading. With Windows 10, you can have many desktops and each desktop is its own virtual space that can span multiple displays. This means the days when Windows was fixed with a single desktop are gone—finally!

Figure 2 shows a desktop with the default configuration. As you can see from the figure, Microsoft revised and refined the taskbar. The Start button opens the Start Menu. For ease of reference, I may sometimes refer to this button simply as Start, as in click Start to open the Start menu.

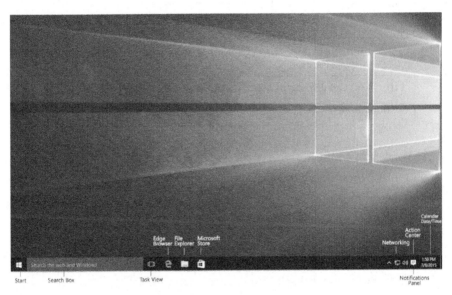

Figure 2 Use the desktop to organize your work.

While clicking Start opens the Start Menu, right-clicking Start displays the shortcut menu shown in Figure 3. Click any of the options on the shortcut menu to open the related tool. Click Shut Down Or Sign Out to display additional options for shutting down the computer, entering sleep mode and signing out.

> **Tip**   An even quicker way to log out? Press Windows logo key + L.

Programs and Features
Power Options
Event Viewer
System
Device Manager
Network Connections
Disk Management
Computer Management
Command Prompt
Command Prompt (Admin)

Task Manager
Control Panel
File Explorer
Search
Run

Shut down or sign out   >
Desktop

Figure 3 Get quick access to commonly used options and features.

> **Tip**   You can also display the shortcut menu by pressing the Windows logo key + X.

In the default configuration, the shortcut menu has options for opening the Command Prompt as a standard user or as an administrator. You can modify Start Menu properties to replace these menu items with options for working with Windows PowerShell by following these steps:

1. Right-click an open area on the taskbar and then select Properties.

2. In the Properties dialog box, select the Navigation tab.

3. On the Navigation tab, select the Replace Command Prompt with Windows PowerShell... option and then click OK.

Cortana & Search

The Search box allows you to quickly and easily search Settings, Control Panel, personal files, apps and the web. To use the search feature, simply start typing when the Start menu is open or click in the Search box and then start typing.

As Figure 4 shows, the first time you use search, you'll have the option of configuring Cortana as your virtual assistant. If you want to set up Cortana, click Next and follow the prompts. Otherwise, click Not Interested and proceed with your search.

> **Note**   If you don't configure Cortana and want to use this feature later, simply click in the Search box, click the Gear icon to access Search Settings and then set Cortana Can Give You Suggestions... to Off by clicking it. This will take you back to the prompt shown in Figure 3, allowing you to configure Cortana.

Figure 4 Use Cortana to assist you and provide helpful reminders.

Whether you use Cortana or not, search with Windows 10 is much more intelligent than with Windows 8. Windows 8 was a mess, often showing web results when you really only wanted results from the local computer and not being clear about where results were coming from. Windows 10 fixes this (mostly). In Figure 5, I entered "display" as my search. Here, the standard search results show related utilities first, settings next and then apps in the Microsoft Store. If you subsequently wanted to search your personal documents, you'd then click My Stuff. Or if you wanted to search the Web instead, you'd then click Web.

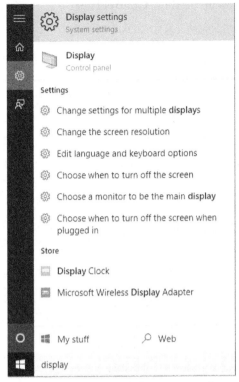

Figure 5 Get smarter, better search results with Windows 10.

Although online and web results are included by default in search results, you can easily change this option so that results only come from Settings, Control Panel, personal files, and apps. Simply click in the Search box, click the Gear icon to access Search Settings and then set Search Online... to Off by clicking it.

As you might expect, there are many more options for search and many powerful parameters you can use to tailor your searches.

Real World The first time you sign in Windows will prepare your environment and there'll be a slight delay before you can start working. Once you can access the desktop, Windows keeps working in the background to set up your environment and part of this process include creating the search indexes for Settings, Control Panel, personal files, and apps.

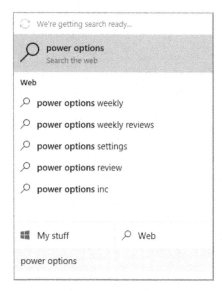

As the graphic shows, while the indexes are being created, you won't get the expected search results and Windows will display a message about getting search ready.

Task View & Changing Desktops

Click the Task View button to display the Task View panel or press the Windows logo key + Tab. As Figure 6 shows, the Task View panel shows a preview of each desktop and allows you to easily add, remove or switch between desktops. With this panel open, you can:

- Add a desktop simply by clicking the New Desktop option. Although you can have many desktops, the desktop space is more manageable when you have between one and nine desktops.
- Switch between desktops simply by clicking the desktop you want to open.

- Delete a desktop simply by right-clicking it and then selecting the Delete button (an X in the upper right corner of the desktop preview).

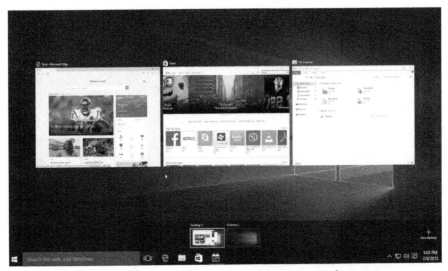

Figure 6 Use the Task View panel to switch between and manage your desktops.

4. Meet the New Start Menu

The Start Menu in Windows 10 combines the best features of the Start Menu used in Windows 7 with the best features of the Start menu used in Windows 8. As Figure 7 shows, the Start Menu features two columns of options. In the first column, you have quick access to the most used apps.

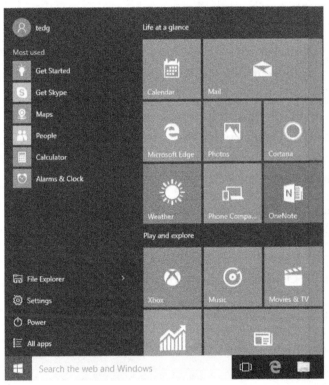

Figure 7 Use the Start Menu to access your apps and options.

> **Tip** "Life at a Glance" and "Play and Explore" are editable headings for the two primary tile regions. To change these headings, simply click the heading to enable editing, make the appropriate changes and then click somewhere else on the Start menu. For example, you can delete "Life at a Glance" and enter "Now Playing" as the heading.

New Tricks for an Old Dog

In the upper left corner of the Start menu, the user name for the currently logged on user is displayed. Click the name to display an options menu that allows you to change account settings, lock the account or sign out.

In the lower left corner of the Start menu, you'll find additional options, including

- **File Explorer**   Opens File Explorer, which replaces Windows Explorer as the utility for exploring your computer. You can open File Explorer quickly by pressing Windows logo key + E.
- **Settings**   Opens the Settings panel. Settings replaces Control Panel for managing most configuration settings. Open Settings quickly by pressing Windows logo key + I.
- **Power**   Displays the power options.

> **Tip**   By default, File Explorer opens with Quick Access selected in the main pane. If you'd rather have File Explorer open with This PC selected, click Options on the View toolbar and then select Change Folder And Search Options. Next, in the Folder Options dialog box, select This PC as the option for the Open File Explorer To list.

The available power options depend on how you are logged in. When you are logged in directly, you can select:

- **Restart**   Shuts down and then restarts the computer
- **Sleep**   Puts the computer in sleep mode, if possible given the system configuration and state.
- **Shut Down**   Shuts down the computer.

> **Note**   If you want to lock the computer or log out instead, click Start, click your user name on the Start menu and then click Lock or Sign Out as appropriate.

More, More, More

If you are logged in remotely, such as when you are accessing a home computer from work, you only have the option to disconnect. Keep in mind your computer's power configuration determines how sleep mode works. When working with sleep mode, it is important to remember that the computer is still drawing power and that you should never open the case or back cover when a Windows 10 device is in the sleep state. Always power off the device before poking around inside the cover.

In the lower left corner, you'll also find the All Apps button which displays the All Apps list (see Figure 8).

Figure 8 Use the All Apps list to find apps you want to open.

As shown in Figure 8, the All Apps list contains a 0-9 A-Z list of available apps. When shown, the list replaces the items in the first column, allowing you to click any entry to open the related app or to click Back to go back to the standard view. Slide or scroll to see the entire list.

The second column on the Start menu shows tiles for apps pinned to Start. Any app on the computer can have a tile on the Start menu. Clicking a tile runs the app. When you right-click a tile, you display configuration options. As shown in Figure 9, you can use these options to:

- Unpin the app from Start
- Change the size of the tile on the Start menu
- Turn live tiles on or off
- Pin the app to the taskbar

Figure 9 Use the options to manage the tile.

Although the previous examples, show the tiles with the live feature turned off, just about any tile can have its live featured turned on, which then displays current information from the app, such as the current weather for the Weather app, the current news heading for the News app or a stock market report for the Stock app.

5. Conquering the Kangaroos

The desktop is what you see after you start your computer and log on. It's your virtual workspace, and you must master it to begin using your computer faster and smarter.

Optimizing Interface Performance

Windows 10 supports visual effects animations, fades and translucent selection rectangles. The Windows 10 desktop with these features enabled is pretty, but like any cosmetic, their value depends on many factors.

On older or less powerful devices, you will want to use less of the pretty stuff; using fewer system resources makes Windows more responsive. The same is likely to be true for that new netbook or tablet PC you just bought.

You can optimize the desktop for the way you want to work by following these steps:

1. Type **SystemPropertiesAdvanced** in the Search box, and then press Enter to open the System Properties dialog box with the Advanced tab selected. (You can get to the same dialog box through Control Panel as well. Click System And Security and then click System. In the left pane, click Advanced System Settings.)

> **Tip** Although there are many shortcuts you can use to access the various tabs and options of the System Properties dialog box, you need not know or remember them all. Instead, pick one technique you like, put it to memory, and use it. The technique I like most is the one mentioned in this step. If the Advanced tab isn't the one I want to work with after I've opened the dialog box, I simply click the tab I want to use, rather than trying to remember that

SystemPropertiesComputerName opens the Computer Name tab, SystemPropertiesHardware opens the Hardware tab, SystemPropertiesProtection opens the System Protection tab, and SystemPropertiesRemote opens the Remote tab.

Real World If command memorization isn't your thing but you'd still like a quick and easy way to access System Properties, try this: Type **SystemPropertiesAdvanced** in the Search box. Right-click SystemPropertiesAdvanced in the results, and then click Open File Location. In File Explorer, right-click SystemPropertiesAdvanced and then select Pin To Taskbar. Now the System Properties | Advanced Tab shortcut is available on the taskbar. Whenever you want to access it, simply click the related icon on the taskbar.

2. In the Performance section, click Settings to open the Performance Options dialog box, shown in Figure 10. You can now:

- Select Adjust For Best Performance to get rid of all the pretty stuff, or select Adjust For Best Appearance to enable all the pretty stuff.
- Select or clear individual visual effects.

3. Save your changes by clicking OK twice to close both dialog boxes.

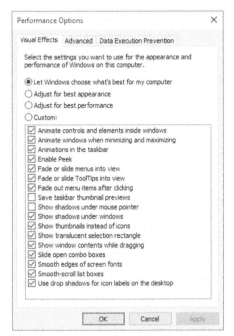

Figure 10 Configuring visual effects to optimize the desktop for the way you want to use it.

The visual add-ons that have the biggest effect on performance include:

- **Animate Controls And Elements Inside Windows**   Controls the slow-fade effect on buttons and tabs in dialog boxes. When off, buttons glow and tabs open without animation.

- **Animate Windows When Minimizing And Maximizing**   Determines whether squeezing or stretching animation is used when minimizing or maximizing windows. When off, Windows pop into position.

- **Animations In the Taskbar**   Controls animations associated with jump lists, thumbnail previews, and sliding taskbar buttons. When off, no animations are used.

- **Fade Or Slide Menus Into View**   Controls whether menus fade or slide into view. When off, menus snap open without delay.

- **Fade Or Slide ToolTips Into View**   Controls whether tooltips fade or slide into view. When off, tooltips snap open without delay.

- **Fade Out Menu Items After Clicking**   Controls whether menu items fade out after clicking. When off, the item selected opens without delay.
- **Slide Open Combo Boxes**   Controls the animations associated with drop-down list boxes. When off, drop-down lists snap open.

Mastering Desktop Essentials

Like a real workspace, the desktop can get cluttered. Programs that you run and folders that you open appear on the desktop in separate windows, and all these open windows can quickly make it difficult to get to the desktop itself. To quickly declutter, you can rearrange open program and folder windows by right-clicking an empty area of the taskbar and then clicking one of the following viewing options:

- **Cascade Windows**   Arranges the open windows so that they overlap, with the title bar remaining visible.
- **Show Windows Stacked**   Resizes the open windows and arranges them on top of each other, in one or more columns.
- **Show Windows Side by Side**   Resizes the open windows and stacks them side by side.

To get to the desktop without decluttering, use the small, blank button on the far right of the taskbar. This button is called the Show Desktop button. You can temporarily hide all open windows by clicking the Show Desktop button. Click the button again to unhide the windows and restore them to their previous state. Alternatively, right-click the taskbar and select Show The Desktop or Show Open Windows as appropriate.

> **Tip**   Another way to hide or show open windows is to press the Windows logo key+D.

The Task View is also handy for working with the desktop. As I told you earlier, you use Task View to add, remove and switch between desktops. When you click the Task View button, you see a preview of each open window on the active desktop, as shown in Figure 11.

In the Task View preview mode, you can:

- Bring any window to the front simply by clicking on it.
- Close any window by hovering over it and then clicking the close button in the upper right corner of the window.

> **Note**   You hover by moving the mouse pointer over a screen element. If you must hover and click, you move the mouse over the element and then click the button or option. With a touch screen, you simply need to tap the element and then tap the button or option.

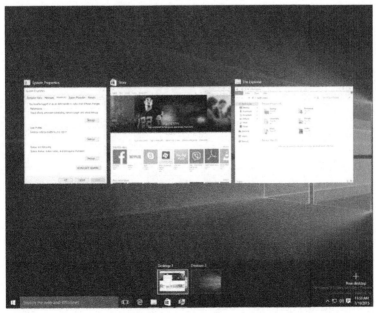

Figure 11 The Task View shows a preview of windows open on the active desktop.

You can store files, folders, and shortcuts on the desktop for quick and easy access. Any file or folder that you drag from a File Explorer window to the desktop stays on the desktop. Rather than placing files or folders on the desktop, you can add a shortcut to a file or folder to the desktop by following these steps:

1. Click the File Explorer icon on the taskbar to use File Explorer to locate the file or folder that you want to add to the desktop.
2. Right-click the file or folder. On the shortcut menu, point to Send To, and then click Desktop (Create Shortcut).

You can also add system icons to the desktop. By default, the only system icon on the desktop is the Recycle Bin. You can add or remove system icons by completing the following steps:

1. Right-click an empty area of the desktop, and then click Personalize.
2. In the left pane of the Personalization window, click Themes and then in the main pane under Related Settings, click Desktop Icon Settings. This opens the Desktop Icon Settings dialog box, as shown in Figure 12.
3. Add or remove icons by selecting or clearing their related check boxes and then clicking OK to save your changes.

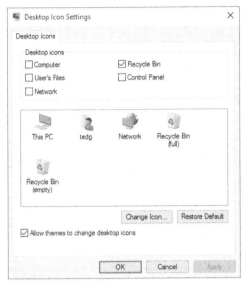

Figure 12 Add or remove desktop icons.

Some of the desktop icons can be renamed by right-clicking the icon, clicking Rename, typing the desired name, and then pressing Enter. For example, you could rename Recycle Bin as Trash Barrel by right-clicking Recycle Bin, clicking Rename, typing Trash Barrel, and then pressing Enter.

If you no longer want an icon or shortcut on the desktop, right-click it, and then click Delete. When prompted, confirm the action by clicking Yes. Each icon has special options and uses:

- **Accessing computers and devices on your network**   Double-clicking the Network icon opens a window where you can access the computers and devices on your network.
- **Accessing Control Panel**   Double-clicking the Control Panel icon opens the Control Panel, which provides access to system configuration and management tools.
- **Accessing hard disks and devices**   Double-clicking the This PC icon opens a window from which you can access hard disk drives and devices with removable storage.

- **Accessing the System page in Control Panel**   Right-clicking the This PC icon and clicking Properties displays the System page in Control Panel.
- **Accessing File Explorer**   Double-clicking the folder icon for the user's files opens your user profile folder in File Explorer.
- **Connecting to network drives**   Right-clicking the This PC icon (or the Network icon) and selecting Map Network Drive allows you to connect to shared network folders.
- **Managing your computer**   Right-clicking the This PC icon and clicking Manage opens the Computer Management console.
- **Removing deleted items**   Right-clicking the Recycle Bin icon and clicking Empty Recycle Bin permanently removes all items in the Recycle Bin.
- **Restoring deleted items**   Double-clicking the Recycle Bin icon opens the Recycle Bin, which you can use to view or restore deleted items.

Now that you know how to add items to the desktop, try this:

1. Create a custom Show Desktop button that you can place anywhere on the desktop, open Notepad.exe, type the commands below, and then save the file on the desktop as Show.scf.

```
[Shell]
Command=2
IconFile=Explorer.exe,3
[Taskbar]
Command=ToggleDesktop
```

2. Now double-click the related icon to display or hide windows on the active desktop.

Stretching the Desktop

Increasingly, desktop PCs and laptops support multiple display devices, allowing you to add a monitor to increase your desktop space. Not only is this a relatively inexpensive way to make your computer more useful, it can also boost your productivity.

Here's an example: You connect two monitors to your computer, or add a monitor as an additional output for your laptop. By placing the screens side by side and enabling multiple displays, you effectively stretch your desktop space and make it possible to view programs and files open on both screens at the same time. This allows you to have multiple windows open all the time— some on your primary screen and some on your secondary screen.

As Windows 10 supports multiple desktops, each of these multiple desktops would also then stretch across the multiple displays. Here, the desktops provide the virtual space and the displays provide the physical space.

Typically, if a computer supports multiple displays, it has multiple display adapter connectors. For example, if a desktop PC has three display adapter connectors (two digital and one analog), it likely supports at least two monitors; if a laptop has additional display adapter connectors (digital or analog), it likely supports at least two monitors.

You can confirm the number of supported displays by checking the technical specifications for your display adapter on the manufacturer's website. To determine the type of display adapter on your computer, right-click an empty area of the desktop, and then click Screen Resolution. On the Screen Resolution page, click the Advanced Settings link. The adapter type listed for your display adapter shows the manufacturer name and model information, such as NVIDIA GeForce GTX 980.

Getting a computer that supports multiple monitors to stretch the desktop across two monitors is best handled as follows:

1. With the computer shut down (and not in the sleep or hibernate state), connect the monitors to the computer, and then turn on the monitors.

2. Next, start your computer and log on.

> **Troubleshooting**　The logon screen should appear on one of the monitors (although not necessarily on the one directly in front of you). If the logon screen doesn't appear, turn off both monitors in turn, and then turn the monitors back on. If a monitor has multiple modes, such as analog and digital, wait for the monitor to switch to the appropriate mode or manually configure the mode by using the monitor's configuration settings. You may need to wiggle the mouse or press keys on the keyboard to get the monitor to sense the appropriate mode.

3. Right-click an open area on the desktop, and then click Display Settings to open the Display page in Settings, shown in Figure 13.

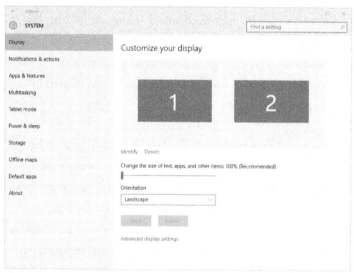

Figure 13 Identify and orient the displays

4. Click Detect to have Windows display the identity number of each monitor. With two monitors, the displays are numbered 1 and 2. By default, Display 1 always includes the Start menu, taskbar, and notification tray, but you can change this as discussed in "Making the Taskbar Dance."

5. Confirm the display order. Windows doesn't know how you've placed the monitors on your desktop. Instead, it assumes that the primary display device is the first one connected and the secondary display device is the second one connected. It also assumes that the second display is to the right of the first display, which allows you to move the mouse pointer to the right to go from the desktop on the first display to the desktop stretched to the second display.

6. You can tell windows how your monitors are oriented in several ways. If Display 2 is on the left side of Display 1, click the representation of the Display 2 desktop on the Screen Resolution page, drag it to the left past the Display 1 desktop, release the mouse button, and then click Apply. The orientation should now show Display 1 on the left and Display 2 on the right; you can confirm proper configuration by clicking the Identify button. To reverse this procedure, perform the same steps, but drag to right instead of to the left.

> **Real World**   If you identify and orient the displays incorrectly, moving from the desktop on one monitor to the stretched desktop on the other monitor won't be logical. For example, if Display 2 is physically located to the right of Display 1, but you've incorrectly configured the displays, you may not be able to access the stretched desktop on Display 2 by moving the pointer to the right. Instead, you may need to move the pointer to the left, past the edge of Display 1's desktop, and vice versa.

After you've connected an additional monitor and oriented it properly, working with multiple monitors is fairly straightforward. When you stretch the desktop across two displays, the resolution setting of both displays determines how large the desktop is. If Display 1's resolution is 1920 x 1080 and Display 2's resolution is 1920 x 1080, the effective resolution is 3840 x 1080.

When you maximize windows, they fill their current display from edge to edge. You can click on windows and drag them from the desktop on one display to the stretched desktop on another display. After you click and drag a window, size it as appropriate for the way you want to use it. For many programs, Windows remembers where you've positioned a window when you close it; the next time you open the window, it appears positioned on the appropriate display, as you last worked with it. However, some programs won't remember your preferred monitor, either by design or because the program isn't appropriate for multiple displays.

Any wallpaper you've selected as the background for your desktop will appear on all your displays. Whether you choose a picture position of Fill, Fit, Stretch, or Center, you see a duplicate of the background on each display.

If you want different pictures to appear on each display, you must create pictures at the appropriate resolution, store them in an appropriate folder (such as a subfolder of C:\Windows\Web\Wallpaper), select them as your desktop background, and use the Span or Tile option of the Choose A Fit list. For example, if Display 1's resolution is 1920 x 1080 and Display 2's resolution is 1920 x 1080, using an art program such as Photoshop, you could combine two 1920 x 1080 images to create one 3840 x 1080 image. You would then store this image in an appropriate folder and select it as your tiled or spanned wallpaper.

The standard screensavers that come with Windows also stretch across your displays automatically. There's no need to do anything special to make this happen.

Ready to Ditch Snap?

Theoretically, you use snap to arrange windows side by side. Here is how snap is supposed to work:

1. If you want two windows to appear side by side on the desktop, you drag the title bar of the first window to the left or right side of the screen until an outline of the expanded window appears, then release the mouse to expand the window.

2. Afterward, you drag the title bar of the second window to the opposite side of the screen until an outline of the expanded window appears, then release the mouse to expand the second window.

3. To return the window to its original size, you simply drag the title bar away from the top of the desktop and then release.

Personally though, snap is always doing what I don't want it to when I use that technique. The only technique that actually works reliably for me is when I snap windows using the keyboard. To snap the active window to the side of the desktop using the keyboard, press either Windows logo key + Left Arrow or Windows logo key + Right Arrow. After you do this, you'll be in Task View and can snap the second window to the opposite side of the screen simply by clicking it.

For easy reference, the keyboard shortcuts for snap are as follows:

- **Windows key + Left Arrow or Right Arrow**   Toggles the screen snap position of the app. Snap splits the screen, so if the app is being displayed normally, Windows key + Left Arrow snaps it to the left and Windows key + Right Arrow snaps it to the right.
- **Windows key + Up Arrow**   Displays the app in Full Screen mode.
- **Windows key + Down Arrow**   Exits Full Screen mode and returns the app to its original window state.

All of these snap behaviors are configurable and controlled with System Settings by following these steps:

1. Click Start and then click Settings.
2. In the Settings dialog box, click System. On the System page, click Multitasking.
3. In the main pane, under Snap, use these options to manage the way snap works:

- If you don't want to use snap, you can disable the feature by toggling the Arrange Windows Automatically... option to the Off position.
- If you don't want to use snap to display two windows side by side, you can disable the feature by toggling the When I Snap More Than One Window... option to the Off position.
- If you don't want snap to show what window you can snap next after you snap a window, you can disable the feature by toggling the When I Snap A Window, Show... option to the Off position.

6. Making the Start Menu Your B*tch

The Start button provides access to your computer's menu system. You open the Start menu simply by clicking the Start button. You also can display the Start menu by pressing the Windows logo key on your keyboard, or by pressing Control+Esc.

As you probably know, the Start menu allows you to run apps, open folders, search your computer, get help, and more. What you may not know is how to customize the Start menu so that it works the way you want it to.

> **Tip** Use Search to quickly run any installed program, system utility or get to system settings. Simply type the program, utility or option name in the Search box. Results for programs, system utilities and system settings are displayed before other types of search results.

By default, the Start menu looks similar to the example shown in Figure 14. Here, you have two columns of entries, with settings and options on the left and apps on the right. In the lower left corner, note the following options:

- File Explorer
- Settings
- All Apps

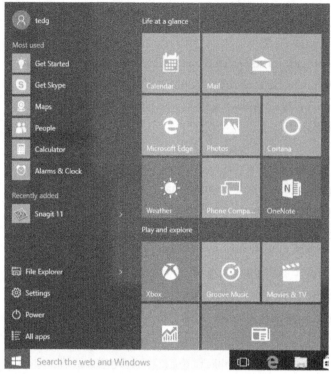

Figure 14 Make the most of Start by customizing it.

File Explorer and Settings are two of many options that can appear in this area of the menu. While these options are enabled by default, many other options, including those for Documents, Downloads, Music and Pictures, are disabled by default. To control which of these options are displayed, follow these steps:

1. Click Start and then click Settings. In the Settings dialog box, click Personalization.

2. On the Personalization page, select Start in the left column.

3. In the main pane, click the Choose Which Folders Appear on Start link. This opens the Choose Which Folders page, as shown in Figure 15.

4. Enable or disable specific options by clicking the related On/Off switch. For example, if the Music switch is off, click the toggle under Music to set the switch to the On position.

Figure 15 Enable or disable folders on the Start menu

Keep in mind that All Apps isn't an option you can turn on or off. If you click All Apps when you are working with Start, you see a scrollable list of all the apps installed on the device in the leftmost column of the Start menu.

Scroll through the list and you'll see folders that store lists of related tools, including folders for Windows Accessories, Windows Administrative Tools, Windows System and more. Click the folder to expand or hide its contents.

Pinning Apps and Using Full-Screen Mode

You can pin an app to Start by following these steps:

1. On the Start menu, click the All Apps option, and then locate the app in the list.

2. Right-click the app in the list and select Pin To Start.

> **Real World**   Sometimes the program you want to pin is not readily accessed in the menu system. In this case, locate the application's

executable file (.exe) in File Explorer. Right-click the file, and then click Pin To Start.

By default, as shown in Figure 16, apps you pin are added to a third section under the "Life At a Glance" and "Play And Explore" sections. You can customize the apps lists by pinning items to the Start menu, resizing Start, creating new sections and more. The first customization trick you need to learn is the art of creating sections.

Figure 16 Pin apps to the Start menu for quick access.

As an alternative to using the popup Start menu, you can use Start in full-screen mode, which is similar to the Start screen in Windows 8. In full-screen mode, items in the left hand column are hidden until you click one of the available buttons. Specifically, you must click the button in the upper left corner to view the standard sidebar and its options.

To enable or disable full-screen mode for Start, follow these steps:

1. Click Start and then click Settings. In the Settings dialog box, click Personalization.
2. On the Personalization page, select Start in the left column.
3. Enable or disable full-screen mode by clicking the related On/Off switch.

Creating Sections

As mentioned previously, when you pin apps to Start, they are added to a new section by default. Windows 10 will in fact let you create many new sections. You create a new section simply by dragging a tile into an empty area. When you drag the tile to a new area, Windows will highlight the area to let you know you a new section will be created.

As with the default sections, each new section can be named. To name a section, complete these steps:

1. Move the mouse cursor over an empty area above the tiles in the section to display the Name Group option and then click. (With a touch screen, simply tap this area)
2. The cursor changes to an insertion point. Type the desired heading and then press Enter or click elsewhere.

If you want an app you've pinned to appear in one of the two standard sections, simply click and drag the app tile to the section you want it to be in. Windows 10 will resize the section automatically to accommodate the addition or removal of tiles. You can use the same click and drag technique to move tiles from one section to another.

Resizing and Reorganizing Tiles

Often after you move tiles around, you'll want to optimize the tile size. To resize a tile, right-click it, point to Resize and then select the desired size. Standard tiles can be set to small or medium size. Tiles capable of displaying live contents, live tiles, can be set:

- Small—70x70 pixels, four small tiles fill the same space as one medium.
- Medium—150x150 pixels, the standard tile size
- Wide—310x150 pixels, a tile that is two medium tiles wide.
- Large—310x310 pixels, one large tile fills the same space as four mediums.

See Figure 17 for examples. The default tile size is medium, which is standard block size.

Figure 17 Size tiles to personalize available space on the Start menu.

While you are adding tiles and moving them around Start, you may want to resize the menu. To change the default height of Start, click and drag the top edge. Drag up to increase the height; drag down to decrease the height. To change the default width of Start, click and drag the right edge. Drag right to increase the width; drag left to decrease the width.

Customizing the Most Used and Recently Added Lists

On the Start menu, the most used and recently added apps are listed in the upper left (unless you change personalization settings, see Figure 18).

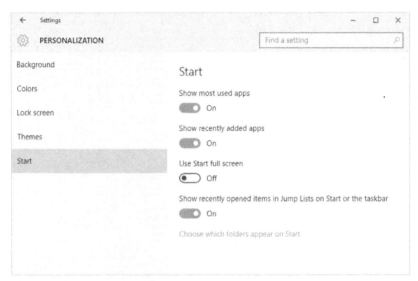

Figure 18 Use Personalization settings to customize start.

You can remove a program from the most used list by right-clicking it and then clicking Don't Show In This List. However, this won't prevent the program from being added to the list in the future.

You can turn the most used and recently added lists on or off by completing the following steps:

1. Click Start and then click Settings.

2. In the Settings dialog box, click Personalization. On the Personalization page, select Start in the left column. This displays the Personalization page.

3. Enable or disable the Show Most Used Apps list by clicking the related On/Off switch.

4. Enable or disable the Show Recently Added Apps list by clicking the related On/Off switch.

7. Making the Taskbar Dance

You use the taskbar to manage your apps and open windows. The taskbar displays buttons for pinned and open items that allow you to quickly access items you've opened and start applications.

Putting the Taskbar Where You Want It

By default, the taskbar is always displayed along the bottom of the desktop on your primary monitor. If you want to move the taskbar to another location, first make sure it's not locked. To do this, right-click the taskbar to display the taskbar options shown in Figure 19.

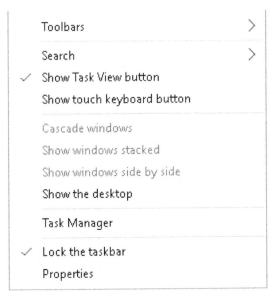

Figure 19 Use the Taskbar options to control basic settings.

> **Note**   If you're using Windows 10 on a tablet PC, see "Entering and Exiting Tablet Mode" for details on change the way the taskbar works in tablet mode.

A checkmark beside the Lock The Taskbar option indicates the taskbar is locked and can't be moved. To unlock the taskbar, right-click it and clear the Lock The Taskbar option by clicking it (which should remove the checkmark).

After you unlock the taskbar, you can position it wherever you want by clicking on it and dragging. You can:

- Drag the taskbar to the left or right to dock it on the left or right side of the primary desktop. Drag up to dock the taskbar to the top of the primary desktop.
- Dock the taskbar to a location on another monitor. Simply drag the taskbar to the desired left, right, top, or bottom location on the stretched desktop.

After you position the taskbar where you want it, you should lock it in position. To do this, right-click an open area of the taskbar, and then select the Lock The Taskbar option. A check mark indicates that it is locked.

Real World   On stretched desktops, you create a desktop that stretches across multiple displays, such as when your computer has two monitors, and the taskbar only appears on your primary monitor. If you'd like the taskbar to appear on the primary monitor and secondary monitors, follow these steps:

1. Click Start and then click Settings.

2. In the Settings dialog box, click System. On the System page, click Multitasking.

3. In the main pane, under Virtual Desktops, select All Desktops as the option for On The Taskbar, Show...

Customizing Taskbar Appearance

You can customize the taskbar in several other ways. The first, by right-clicking it and using the options available, including:

- **Show Task View Button**   Controls the display of the Task View button. If you clear this option, you'll hide the Task View button and won't be able to use Task View or add, remove or switch between desktops.
- **Toolbars**   Controls the display of the toolbars that can be added to the taskbar. The standard toolbars are Address, Links and Desktop. You also can select New Toolbar to choose a folder to add as a toolbar.

You can customize other aspects of the taskbar by using the Taskbar And Start Menu Properties dialog box, shown in Figure 20.

Figure 20 Use the Properties dialog box to customize the taskbar appearance.

To access this dialog box, right-click an open area of the taskbar, and then click Properties. Select or clear options as desired and click OK to save your changes.

The available options include:

- **Lock The Taskbar**   Locks the taskbar in place to prevent accidental moving or resizing. You must clear this option to move or resize the taskbar.
- **Auto-Hide The Taskbar**   Hides the taskbar when you aren't using it and displays the taskbar only when you move the cursor over it. If you clear this option, the taskbar is always displayed (although not always on top), which you may prefer, especially if you move the taskbar around a stretched desktop.

> **Tip**   If the taskbar is hidden and you forget where it is docked, you can quickly display the taskbar and Start menu by pressing the Windows logo key.

- **Use Small Taskbar Buttons**   Reduces the size of taskbar buttons, allowing more buttons to fit on the taskbar. On my desktop PC, I prefer large icons, which makes them easier to click, but on my tablet PC, I prefer small icons so they take up less screen space.
- **Taskbar Location On Screen**   Sets the relative location of the taskbar on the currently targeted display. As we discussed previously, you can move the taskbar manually as well when it is unlocked.
- **Taskbar Buttons**   Specifies whether taskbar buttons are always combined, combined only when the taskbar is full, or never combined.

See the next section for more information on combining buttons and using related options.

> **Note**   Typically, you'll want to combine similar items to reduce taskbar clutter. Rather than displaying a button for each program, the

taskbar groups similar buttons by default. Grouping buttons saves room on the taskbar and helps reduce the likelihood that you'll need to expand the taskbar to find the buttons for open programs.

Pinning Programs to the Taskbar

You can pin items that you work with frequently to the taskbar. Pinning an item to the taskbar creates a shortcut that allows you to quickly open a program, folder, or related window.

Pinning items is easy. If you know the name of the program you want to pin to the taskbar, start typing the program name into the Search box. When you see the program in the results list, right-click it, and then click Pin To Taskbar. From this point on, whenever you want to access the program, simply click the related icon on the taskbar.

Another way to find items to pin is to access the Start menu, and then click the All Apps button. When you find the program you want to pin, right-click the program's menu item, and then click Pin To Taskbar.

To remove a pinned program from the taskbar, right-click its icon, and then click Unpin This Program From The Taskbar. This removes the program's button from the taskbar.

You can set the order of buttons for all opened and pinned programs. To do this, click the button on the taskbar and drag it left or right to the desired position.

When buttons are combined on the taskbar, clicking an item with multiple windows displays a thumbnail with a representation of each open window. You can hover over a window to peek at it on the desktop (as long as the appropriate Aero features are enabled) or click a window that you want to work with to open it. For example, if you open three different folders in File Explorer, these items are grouped together in one taskbar button. Hovering over the taskbar button displays a thumbnail with an entry for each window, allowing you to select the grouped window to open by clicking it.

Taskbar buttons make it easy to close windows as well. To close a window, whether grouped or not, move the pointer over the related taskbar button. When the thumbnail appears, move the mouse pointer to the right, and then click the close button for the window you want to close.

Using Flip Views and Jump Lists

Flip views and jump lists are some of the most powerful features of Windows 10. Why? They allow you to quickly get to items that you want to work with.

Display the standard flip view by pressing Alt+Tab. As shown in Figure 21, the flip view contains live thumbnails of all open windows, which are continuously updated to reflect their current state. You can work with a flip view in a variety of ways. Here are a few techniques:

- Press Alt+Tab, and then hold Alt to keep the flip view open.
- Press Tab while you hold the Alt key to cycle through the windows.
- Release the Alt key to bring the currently selected window to the front.
- Select a window and bring it to the front by clicking it.

Figure 21 Using the flip view.

By default, flip view shows windows are open only on the active desktop. If you're like me and use several desktops all the time, you may want flip view to show windows that are open on any desktop. To configure this option, follow these steps:

1. Click Start and then click Settings.
2. In the Settings dialog box, click System. On the System page, click Multitasking.
3. In the main pane, under Virtual Desktops, select All Desktops as the option for Pressing Alt + Tab Shows Windows That Are Open On.

If you think flip views are cool, wait until you try jump lists. Jump lists are displayed after a short delay whenever you right-click an item that has been pinned to the taskbar. When a program's jump list is displayed, you can select a file to open or task to perform simply by clicking it.

Most applications display recently used items or frequently used items. Some applications have enhanced jump lists that also provide quick access to tasks that you can perform with the application.

Windows 10 also allows you to pin items to a program's jump list. To do this, drag an item associated with a program to the program's button pinned on the taskbar and release when the Pin To option appears. Consider the following real-world scenario:

- You want to pin Microsoft Word to the taskbar and pin important documents to its jump list. To pin Word to the taskbar, you access the Start menu, type **Word.exe** in the Search box, right-click Word.exe in the results, and then click Pin To Taskbar.
- After pinning Word to the taskbar, you want to add important documents to its jump list. You open File Explorer, locate the first document, drag the document file from the Explorer window to the Word button on the taskbar. When the Pin To Word option appears, you release the mouse button to add the first document to the jump list. You repeat this process to build your list.

Other ways to use jump lists include the following:

- Simply open File Explorer and locate and then drag an important folder from this window to the pinned File Explorer on the taskbar. When the Pin To File Explorer option appears, release the mouse button to add the folder to the jump list. Repeat this process to build your list.
- If you pin Control Panel to the taskbar, you can add frequently used tasks to its jump list. To pin Control Panel to the taskbar, access the Start menu, type **Control Panel** in the Search box, right-click Control Panel in the results, and then click Pin To Taskbar. After you've pinned Control Panel to the taskbar, simply open Control Panel, locate an important task, and then drag the address link for the task to the pinned Control Panel on the taskbar. When the Pin To Control Panel option appears, release the mouse button to add the task to the jump list. Repeat this process to build your list.

> **Real World** Sometimes, you'll want to run programs pinned to the taskbar with administrator privileges. To do this, right-click the shortcut on the taskbar to display the options menu for the program and then in the options list, right-click the program name. If you can run the program with administrator privileges, the second options menu will have a Run As Administrator option which you can select.

8. Customizing Backgrounds

If you really want to express your true self, the desktop background can help you do it. The Windows desktop can display a solid background color or a picture as its wallpaper. Windows 10 provides a starter set of background images that you can use as wallpaper.

To access the Background page, shown in Figure 22, simply right-click on the desktop and click Personalize.

Figure 22 Customizing the desktop background.

The default wallpaper images are stored in subfolders of the %WinDir%\Web\Wallpaper folder, where %WinDir% is an environment variable that points to the base installation folder for Windows such as C:\Windows. For the most part, these images are sized for either widescreen viewing at 1920 x 1200, but there may also be images sized for widescreen viewing on stretched desktops at 3840 x 1200. If you select an image at one of these sizes and your computer monitor has a different display resolution size, Windows resizes the image automatically every time the image is used.

> **Note**   The best pictures for stretched desktops are panoramas, as panoramas are very wide, and when you are working with backgrounds and themes, you'll find backgrounds and themes designed for stretched desktops are often referred to as panoramic backgrounds or panoramic themes.
>
> **Tip**   To remove the overhead associated with background resizing, you can size your background images so that they are the same size as your preferred display resolution. If you do this, however, make sure that you save the re-sized images to a new location and then choose this new location. Don't overwrite the existing images.

You can also create background images to use as wallpaper. To do so, simply create appropriately sized images as .bmp, .gif, .jpg, .jpg, .jpeg, .dib, .png, .tif, or .tiff files, and then add these files to the appropriate subfolders of the %WinDir%\Web\Wallpaper folder. If you do not have access to that folder, or if you would prefer to not make changes to that folder, you can also use pictures from your Pictures Library or elsewhere.

> **Note**   You should optimize every background image you use. If you don't do this, you risk affecting your computer's performance because Windows will need to resize the image every time it is used.

Windows 10 allows you to use three different types of backgrounds:

- Pictures
- Solid Colors
- Slideshows

Using Pictures for Backgrounds

You can set the picture background for the desktop by completing the following steps:

1. Right-click an open area of the desktop, and then click Personalize. In the left column, Background is selected by default, as shown previously in Figure 3-4.
2. On the Background list, choose Picture. Next, click the picture you want to use, or click Browse to select a picture in another location, such as your personal Documents or Pictures folder.
3. When you are using a background image, you must also use the Choose A Fit option to select a display option for the background. The positioning options are:

- **Fill**   Fills the desktop background with the image. Generally, the fill is accomplished by zooming in, which may result in the sides of the image being cropped.
- **Fit**   Fits the image to the desktop background. Because current proportions are maintained in most cases, this is a good option for photos and large images that you want to see without stretching or expanding.
- **Stretch**   Stretches the image to fill the desktop background. The proportions are maintained as closely as possible, and then the height is stretched to fill any remaining gaps.
- **Tile**   Repeats the image so that it covers the entire screen. This is a good option for small images and icons (and also to get a single image to fill two screens, as discussed earlier in "Conquering the Kangaroos."
- **Center**   Centers the image on the desktop background. Any area that the image doesn't fill uses the current desktop background color. Click Change Background Color to set the background color for the area the image doesn't fill.
- **Span**   Allows the image to fill a stretched desktop by spanning the space from one desktop to the other.

Using Solid Colors for Backgrounds

You can set a solid color for the desktop background by completing the following steps:

1. Right-click an open area of the desktop, and then click Personalize. In the left column, Background is selected by default, as shown previously in Figure 3-4.
2. On the Background list, choose Solid Color.
3. Under Background Colors, click the background color that you want to use.

Using Slideshow Backgrounds

With a slideshow, the background image changes automatically based on a specific schedule, such as every 30 minutes or daily. Before you can use a slideshow, however, you need to create a picture album containing the pictures you want to display in the background.

The default picture album is the Pictures library in your personal folders. As pictures in your library likely aren't sized or optimized for the desktop, displaying the images may be rather inefficient in terms of system resource usage. If you want to reduce resource usage, you should optimize the size of images and then copy these to a new folder that you then use as your photo album.

> **Tip** The optimum size of images for your device depends on the display settings. To check the display settings for you device, click Start and then click Settings. In the Settings dialog box, click System. With Display selected in the left pane, scroll down in the main pane and then select Advanced Display Settings. Under Resolution, you'll see the current resolution for the device's display, such as 1280 x 1024 or

1920 x 1200. If you've stretched the desktop on your device and want to create a stretched background, the background size should be 2 times the width of the display. Thus, if the display is 1920 pixels wide, the image should be 3840 pixels wide.

You configure the slideshow for the background by completing the following steps:

1. Right-click an open area of the desktop, and then click Personalize. In the left column, Background is selected by default.

2. On the Background list, choose Slideshow, as shown in Figure 23.

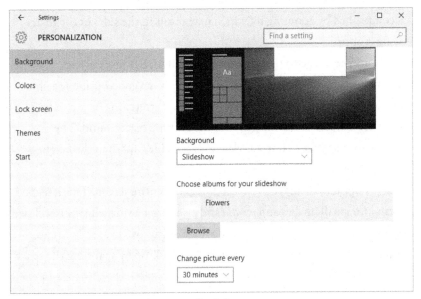

Figure 23 Creating a change schedule.

3. By default, your Pictures library is used as the source album for the slideshow. To use a different source, click Browse to select a picture in another location, such as your personal Documents or Pictures folder.

> **Tip**   If you have administrator access to the device, you can set one of the Windows wallpaper folders as the source. Click Browse, navigate

to the base folder for wallpaper, such as C:\Windows\Web and then choose the folder to use.

4. Use the Change Picture Every list to specify how often pictures should be rotated, such as every 30 minutes, every hour, every 6 hours or every day.

5. You must also select a display option for the background. The positioning options are:

- **Center** Centers the image on the desktop background. Any area that the image doesn't fill uses the current desktop background color. Click Change Background Color to set the background color for the area the image doesn't fill.

- **Fill** Fills the desktop background with the image. Generally, the fill is accomplished by zooming in, which may result in the sides of the image being cropped.

- **Fit** Fits the image to the desktop background. Because current proportions are maintained in most cases, this is a good option for photos and large images that you want to see without stretching or expanding.

- **Stretch** Stretches the image to fill the desktop background. The proportions are maintained as closely as possible, and then the height is stretched to fill any remaining gaps.

- **Tile** Repeats the image so that it covers the entire screen. This is a good option for small images and icons (and also to get a single image to fill two screens, as discussed in "Conquering the Kangaroos.").

- **Span** Allows the image to fill a stretched desktop by spanning the space from one desktop to the other.

9. Customizing Lock Screens

Like the desktop, the lock screen can have a picture or slideshow background. Windows 10 provides a starter set of background images for the lock screen. The default lock screen images are stored in subfolders of the %WinDir%\Web\Screen folder, where %WinDir% is an environment variable that points to the base installation folder for Windows such as C:\Windows.

For the most part, the default images are sized for either widescreen viewing at 1920 x 1200, but there may also be images sized for widescreen viewing on stretched desktops at 3840 x 1200 or larger. If you select an image at one of these sizes and your computer monitor has a different display resolution size, Windows resizes the image automatically every time the image is used.

To access the Lock Screen page, shown in Figure 24, simply right-click on the desktop and click Personalize. Next, on the Personalization page, click Lock Screen in the left column.

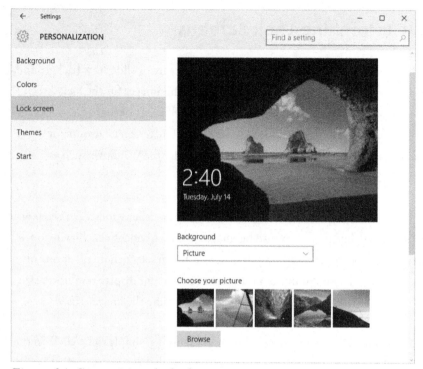

Figure 24 Customizing the lock screen.

Just as you can create background images to use as wallpaper, you can create background images for the lock screen. To do so, simply create appropriately sized images as .bmp, .gif, .jpg, .jpg, .jpeg, .dib, .png, .tif, or .tiff files, and then add these files to the %WinDir%\Web\Screen folder. If you do not have access to that folder, or if you would prefer to not make changes to that folder, you can also use pictures from your Pictures Library or elsewhere.

Windows 10 allows you to use two different types of backgrounds on the lock screen:

- Pictures
- Slideshows

You also can specify apps that can display their status on the lock screen, such as Alarms & Clock, Mail, Weather and Calendar.

Using Pictures on the Lock Screen

You can set the picture for the lock screen by completing the following steps:

1. Right-click an open area of the desktop, and then click Personalize. Next, on the Personalization page, click Lock Screen in the left column.
2. On the Background list, choose Picture. Next, click the picture you want to use, or click Browse to select a picture in another location, such as your personal Documents or Pictures folder.

By default, the picture fills the screen. Generally, the fill is accomplished by zooming in. If you want the picture to fill a stretched desktop by spanning the space from one desktop to the other, you'll need to create a picture that is 2 times the width of the display. Thus, if the display is 1920 pixels wide, the image should be 3840 pixels wide.

Using Slideshows on the Lock Screen

With a slideshow, the image on the lock screen changes automatically every few minutes. Before you can use a slideshow, however, you need to create a picture album containing the pictures you want to display in the background.

The default picture album is the Pictures library in your personal folders. As pictures in your library likely aren't sized or optimized for the lock screen, only pictures that fit the screen are displayed by default. Also by default, when you are using Windows on a desktop or laptop computer, Windows shows the lock screen when the computer is inactive rather than turning off the screen.

> **Tip** The optimum size of images for your device depends on the display settings. To check the display settings for you device, click Start and then click Settings. In the Settings dialog box, click System. With

Display selected in the left pane, scroll down in the main pane and then select Advanced Display Settings. Under Resolution, you'll see the current resolution for the device's display, such as 1280 x 1024 or 1920 x 1200. If you've stretched the desktop on your device and want to create a stretched background, the background size should be 2 times the width of the display. Thus, if the display is 1920 pixels wide, the image should be 3840 pixels wide.

You configure the slideshow for the lock screen by completing the following steps:

1. Right-click an open area of the desktop, and then click Personalize. Next, on the Personalization page, click Lock Screen in the left column.

2. On the Background list, choose Slideshow. By default, your Pictures library is used as the source album for the slideshow. You can now add and remove source albums. If you don't want the Pictures library to be used as a source album (perhaps due to it containing embarrassing photos), click Pictures under Choose Albums... and then click Remove.

3. The photos in each selected album will be used in the slideshow. To use add a source album, click Add A Folder and then select the source folder. To use remove a source album, click the folder under Choose Albums... and then select Remove.

While you're working with slideshows on the lock screen, you may want to configure advanced settings to optimize the way the slideshows work. If so, click the Advanced Slideshow Settings link and then use these options for optimization:

- **Include Camera Roll Folders...**   By default, this option is Off and camera roll folders from your Pictures library and OneDrive aren't included in slideshows. If you want these folders included automatically, click the related toggle to switch it to the On position.

- **Use Only Pictures That Fit My Screen** By default, this option is On and only pictures that are sized appropriately are displayed on the lock screen. If you want to include images regardless of whether they are sized appropriately, click the related toggle to switch it to the Off position.
- **When My PC Is Inactive, Show Lock Screen** By default, this option for desktop and laptop computers is On. This means the lock screen is displayed when the computer is inactive instead of turning off the display. If you want the display to turn off, click the related toggle to switch it to the Off position.

By default, the screen doesn't turn off while the slideshow is playing. To change this behavior, click the Turn Off Screen After... list and then choose a specific turn off time, such as after 30 minutes or after 1 hour.

Configuring Notifications on the Lock Screen

Getting notifications on the lock screen is handy so that you don't have to login to get information you may be looking for, such as whether you have new messages, what the weather is like or what the stock market is doing. Apps that can run in the background and show notifications on the lock screen include:

- Alarms & Clocks, Calendar, Mail
- People, Store, Weather, Xbox

While all of these apps can display short notifications, referred to as quick statuses, only a few apps can display longer, detailed status updates, which for the out-of-the-box apps, includes Weather, Calendar and Xbox.

You can specify apps that can display status updates on the lock screen by completing the following steps:

1. Right-click an open area of the desktop, and then click Personalize. Next, on the Personalization page, click Lock Screen in the left column.

2. In the main pane, scroll down, until you see the status settings shown in Figure 25.

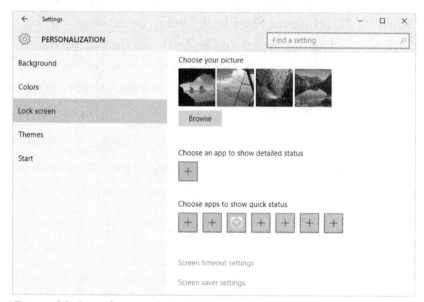

Figure 25 Specify apps that can display status updates on the lock screen.

3. You can configure one app to show detailed status updates on the lock screen. Click Choose An App To Show Detailed Status and then select one of the available apps. If you don't want any app to show a detailed status, select None.

4. Using the Choose Apps To Show Quick Status options, you can configure up to seven apps to show quick status updates on the lock screen. Click one of the available slots and then select an app to display updates in this slow. If you don't want any app to show a quick status in a particular slot, select None.

10. Customizing User Accounts

User accounts have many properties, including a password, a picture, an account name, and an account type designation. You can manage the properties for local accounts, as long as you have an administrator account or the user name and password of an administrator account.

Changing Account Pictures

Your account picture is displayed on the logon screen and on the Start menu. When you use a picture, Windows 10 automatically optimizes the picture and saves the optimized copy as part of your personal Contact entry in Windows Contacts. Although it may seem strange to save the picture as part of your personal .contact file, doing so is a quick and easy shortcut for the operating system. Most pictures are optimized to a file size of 50 KB or less—even high-resolution pictures.

To change your account picture, follow these steps:

1. Click Start and then click Settings. Next, in Settings, click Accounts.
2. As Figure 26 shows, your current account picture (if any) is shown. Click Browse.
3. Use the Open dialog box to choose the picture you want to use. The picture must be in a standard picture format, such as BMP, GIF, JPEG, PNG, DIB, or TIFF.

> **Note** If your computer has a camera, you also can create a picture. Click Camera and follow the prompts.

Figure 26 Choosing a picture for your user account

Changing Account Types

User accounts are either standard user accounts with limited privileges or administrator user accounts with full privileges. As a safety precaution, you might want to use a standard account for web browsing and other online activities and the administrator account only when you need to manage or maintain your computer.

It's common for computers to have multiple users, resulting in several user accounts created on it, and at least one of these must be an administrator account. If you are logged on with a standard user account, you can change the account type to Administrator. If you are logged on with an administrator account, you can change the account type to Standard User (as long as it's not the last administrator account on the computer).

> **Real World**   Ideally, you should create at least two administrator
> accounts on your computer—with passwords. If you forget the

password for one account, you can simply log on with the other account and use the User Accounts options in Control Panel to change your password. But only do this if you've truly lost your password. Why? When you change an account password via another account, you'll lose all EFS-encrypted files, personal certificates, and stored passwords for both websites and network resources.

You can change the account type by following these steps:

1. Type **User Accounts** in the Search box and press Enter. This opens the User Accounts page in Control Panel.

2. Click Manage User Accounts. If you are logged on as a standard user, provide the account name and password of an administrator when prompted and then click Yes.

3. In the User Accounts dialog, double-click the account you want to modify.

4. In the Properties dialog box for the user, on the Group Membership tab, select either Standard User or Administrator and then click OK.

Changing and Recovering Your Password

Periodically, you should change your account password or PIN. This makes it more difficult for someone to gain access to your computer. You can change the standard password, PIN or picture password associated with your user account by following these steps:

1. Click Start and then click Settings. Next, in Settings, click Accounts.

2. On the Accounts page, click Sign-In Options in the left pane.

3. Under Password, PIN or Picture, click Change and then follow the prompts.

If you are using a local account and you've lost or forgotten your password, you can recover and reset your password by following these steps:

1. Using another computer, open a browser window and access https://account.live.com/password/reset.
2. Specify why you can't login as I Forgot My Password, click Next and then follow the prompts.

If you are using a local account and you've lost or forgotten your password, you can use another account to recover (but only if you followed my earlier advice about creating another administrator account). To do so, follow these steps:

1. Type **User Accounts** in the Search box and press Enter. This opens the User Accounts page in Control Panel.
2. Click Manage User Accounts. If you are logged on as a standard user, provide the account name and password of an administrator when prompted and then click Yes.
3. In the User Accounts dialog, click the account you want to modify and then click Reset Password.
4. After you enter and then confirm the new password, click OK. You'll then be able to login using this password.

> **Note** When you change an account password via another account, you'll lose all EFS-encrypted files, personal certificates, and stored passwords for both websites and network resources.

11. Exploring Your Computer in New Ways

There are few components of the Windows operating system that you'll spend more time using than File Explorer. Every time you browse files and folders on your computer, you use File Explorer—whether you specifically open an Explorer window or you use the Open command in an application, such as Microsoft Word. Control Panel, the Computer window, the Network window, and even the Recycle Bin are different views for File Explorer.

Getting There

As Figure 27 shows, File Explorer has an Address bar for quickly navigating disks and folders, a Search box for fast searches, and the following view panes:

- **Navigation**   Helps you quickly access favorites, homegroups, your computer, and your network. Drag any folder to Favorites to quickly create a shortcut to it; right-click and select Remove to delete a favorite.
- **Contents**   Provides the main working pane and shows the contents of your selected drive or folder. Use the View button and View options to control whether item details, lists, or icons are shown.
- **Details**   Shows information about a selected item. The details provided depend on the item selected and are different for drives, folders, documents, songs, videos, and shortcuts. Hide or show the Details pane by clicking Organize, clicking Layout, and then clicking Preview Pane.
- **Preview**   Shows a preview of your selected document, picture, song, video, or other file type, as long as a preview control is available and configured for that file type. Use the Show/Hide Preview button to display or hide the Preview pane.

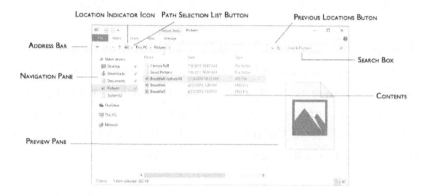

LOCATION INDICATOR ICON   PATH SELECTION LIST BUTTON   PREVIOUS LOCATIONS BUTTON

ADDRESS BAR

NAVIGATION PANE

SEARCH BOX

CONTENTS

PREVIEW PANE

Figure 27 Exploring the drives, folders, and files on your computer.

Microsoft continues to de-emphasize the idea of "library" folders. Libraries are predefined and provide a combined view of folders related to specific types of media, such as Documents, Music and Pictures. Generally, in Windows 10, the only time you work with libraries is when you click the Path Selection List button in File Explorer and select Libraries. Then, as shown in Figure 28, File Explorer specifically states that each item listed is a library.

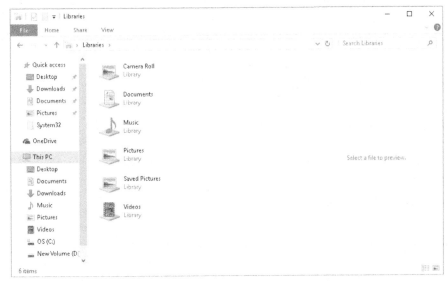

Figure 28 Libraries provide combined views of folders containing similar types of data.

Getting It Done

When you are working with a library, such as the Documents library, you can right-click it and select Properties to get additional information about where that library's data comes from (see Figure 29). You can then use the options provided to add or remove folders from the library, and set default save locations.

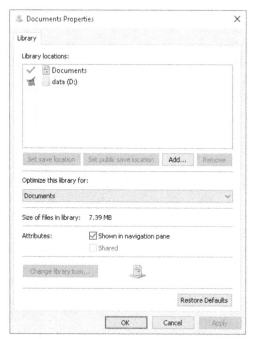

Figure 29 Use the Properties dialog box to manage the library.

Because library data can come from multiple folders, some users have always found libraries a bit confusing. This is why Microsoft is de-emphasizing the feature in favor of the This PC and Quick Access, both of which are available in File Explorer.

When you select This PC as a location or This PC on the navigation pane (see Figure 30), you have fast access to your personal folders, including Documents, Music, Pictures and Videos.

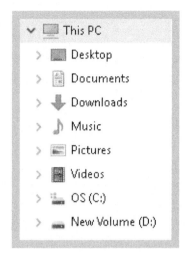

Figure 30 Use This PC to access drives and personal folders.

When Quick Access is expanded on the navigation pane (see Figure 31), you have fast access to any folder or file pinned to this panel. By default, Desktop, Downloads, Documents and Pictures are pinned to Quick Access.

Figure 31 Use Quick Access to access frequently used folders and files.

While working with File Explorer or any of its views, you can add a folder or file to Quick Access by right-clicking it and selecting Pin To Quick Access. To remove a pinned folder or file, right-click it on the Quick Access panel and then select Unpin From Quick Access.

Managing Access History

When you are working with Quick Access, you may find that some folders and files don't have pins. Folders are added by Windows when you use them frequently and files are added when you've recently opened them. Because these items aren't actually pinned, they will be removed automatically when you use them less frequently.

To ensure a folder or file stays available, you can right-click it on the Quick Access panel and then select Pin To Quick Access. To remove an automatically added folder or file, right-click it on the Quick Access panel and then select Remove From Quick Access.

For privacy reasons, you may want to control whether folders and files are added to Quick Access. To do this, follow these steps:

1. In File Explorer, right-click the top of the Quick Access panel and select Options.

2. In the Folder Options dialog box, shown in Figure 32, you'll find options for controlling whether folders and files are added to Quick Access. Use the following techniques to manage Quick Access and then click OK:

- Clear the Show Frequently Used Folders checkbox if you no longer want frequently used folders to be added.
- Clear the Show Recently Used Files checkbox if you no longer want recently used files to be added.
- Click the Clear button to clear the history regarding frequently used folders and files.

Figure 32 Manage Quick Access using Folder Options.

> **Tip** By default, File Explorer opens with Quick Access selected in the main pane. If you'd rather have File Explorer open with This PC selected, select This PC on the Open File Explorer To list.

12. Zeroing in on Apps

Desktop apps are automatically added to Start when you install them and will have a tile. A tile makes it easy to work with the app. Right-click the tile to display management options. Management options depend on the type of tile. Live tiles can update their contents, and these updates can be turned on or off by right-clicking and selecting Turn Live Tile On or Turn Live Tile Off as appropriate. As discussed earlier in "Making the Start Menu Your B*tch," tiles can be displayed in several sizes, and you can make a tile smaller or larger as needed. If you no longer want a tile to be displayed on Start, you can right-click the tile and choose the Unpin From Start option.

If you unpin an app, it's still accessible by clicking the All Apps button. All Apps is the Windows 10 equivalent to the Programs menu in early release of Windows. Windows 10 apps with live tiles start updating immediately after installation. Unlike traditional desktop programs where you typically have only one foreground program, multiple apps can share the screen and remain in the foreground. Apps can open other apps and share the screen with them; one app also can use multiple monitors.

Getting Your Apps

Out of the box, computers running Windows 10 can install only trusted app packages that come from the Windows Store. You can access the Windows Store, shown in Figure 33, using the Store options on Start and the toolbar. If you are logged on to your device with a connected account, you'll be logged into the store automatically and can begin browsing for apps. While you can download any free app without having to provide payment information, the first time you purchase a paid app, you'll need to provide complete details for a credit, debit or other card.

Figure 33 Visiting the Windows Store

Connecting Your Account to the Store

Sometimes you'll be working with a local account or domain account that isn't connected to a Microsoft account. For example, you may prefer not having Microsoft track information about your every online activity and therefore opt not to use a connected account. Don't worry, you can still get apps from the Windows Store.

If you need to login and have an Outlook.com, Hotmail, Live.com, MSN or other valid account in the Microsoft network, follow these steps to get connected to the store:

1. Click Account Options on the toolbar and then click Sign In.

2. When prompted to choose an account, click Microsoft Account.

3. Enter the email address and password for your Microsoft account and then click Sign In.

4. When prompted for your current Windows password, as shown in Figure 34, do one of the following:

- Provide your password and click Next to connect your current account to the Microsoft account and thereafter, you'll need to log in to your Windows device using the Microsoft account and password.
- Specify that you don't want switch to a Microsoft account for login by clicking the Sign In To Just This App Instead link. This option ensures your Microsoft account is used only for signing in to the Store.

Figure 34 Connecting your account

If you need to login and don't have an Outlook.com, Hotmail, Live.com, MSN or other valid account in the Microsoft network, follow these steps to get connected to the store:

1. Click Account Options on the toolbar and then click Sign In.

2. When prompted to choose an account, click the Create One link.

3. Enter your first and last name in the text boxes provided.

4. Next, you are prompted for an email address to use for accessing Microsoft networks. This email address can be your work or home email address, but should be one that only you have access to as it will be the address used for recovering your account and verifying your identity if needed.

> **Tip**   If you don't want to connect an existing email address into the Microsoft network, you can click the Get A New Email Address link and then enter a unique identifier for a new outlook.com email address.

5. Whether you entered your email address or created a new one, you must next enter a password. This password is for accessing the Microsoft network and should not be the same one you use for login or email access.

6. Use the selection lists provided to specify your country of origin and birthdate and then click Next.

7. Protect your account by entering a phone number that can be used to validate your account. Or click the Add An Alternate Email Instead link and then enter an alternate email address. When you are ready to continue, click Next twice.

8. When prompted for your current Windows password, as shown previously in Figure 34, do one of the following:

- Provide your password and click Next to connect your current account to the Microsoft account and thereafter, you'll need to log in to your Windows device using the Microsoft account and password.

- Specify that you don't want switch to a Microsoft account for login by clicking the Sign In To Just This App Instead link. This option ensures your Microsoft account is used only for signing in to the Store.

Finding and Installing Your Apps

Once you are signed in to the Store, you can get and install apps. Browse the store to find apps. Get and install an app, simply by clicking it's purchase button. With free apps, you simply click the Free button. The first time you purchase a paid app, however, you'll need to enter payment information.

Apps that are in the process of being downloaded and installed are shown on the Downloads And Installs page, which is accessed by clicking the Downloads option on the toolbar. If there's a problem downloading and installing an app, you'll see an error, as shown in Figure 35. Get more information about the error by clicking the See Details link. Try to download and install the app again by clicking the Retry option.

Figure 35 Checking the downloads and installs queue.

If you've made previous purchases on other devices, you'll find those purchases in your media library. Click Account Options on the toolbar and then click My Library. Apps that you've purchased but aren't yet installed have a download icon, as shown in Figure 36.

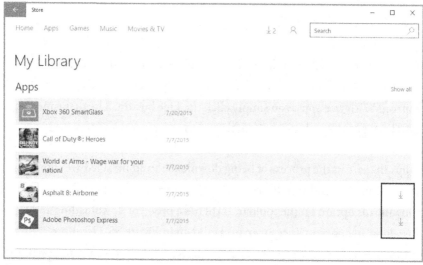

Figure 36 Getting downloads from your library.

By default, apps are updated automatically so you don't have to worry about checking for updates and installing them. While this is usually a good thing, you may not want apps to be updated automatically if you frequently use more costly mobile data instead of wi-fi. If so, you can specify that you don't want apps to be updated automatically by following these steps:

1. Click Account Options and then select Settings.
2. On the Settings page, set Update Apps Automatically to Off by clicking it.
3. If you turn off automatic updates, you'll then need to manually check for updates periodically, by clicking the Downloads option and then clicking the Check For Updates button.

While you are working with Settings, you may also want to specify that the Windows Store app only updates its live tile when you are connected to wi-fi. To do this, set the Only Update The Tile... option to Off.

> **Real World**   When Update Apps Automatically is set to On, Windows 10 checks for updates to all installed apps daily. The daily check occurs every 20 hours. Thus, if the update check starts at 4:00

PM today, it'll start at 12:00 PM tomorrow and 8:00 AM the day after. If this time is missed, Windows 10 performs the check and any subsequent updates as soon as possible after the scheduled start is missed. Although the check and updates occur regardless of whether the computer is running on AC power or battery, Windows 10 won't check for updates when you are using mobile data and will instead wait until you have a wi-fi connection.

Managing Currently Running Apps, Programs and Processes

In Windows 10, you can view and work with your computer's currently running apps, programs and processes by using Task Manager. Open Task Manager by pressing Ctrl+Shift+Esc or by right-clicking the lower-left corner of the screen and then clicking Task Manager on the shortcut menu.

By default, Task Manager displays a summary list of all running apps and programs, as shown in Figure 37.

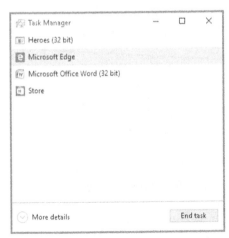

Figure 37 View running apps and programs.

When you click an apps or program in the list, you can manage it. To exit an app or program (which might be necessary when it is not responding), click it in the Task list, and then click End Task. To display other management options, right-click the app or program in the Task list.

When working with the summary view, you can click More Details to open the full Task Manager. You'll then see detailed information about running programs, apps and processes, as shown in Figure 38. The Processes tab lists each item running on the computer under three general headings:

- **Apps**   Shows desktop apps and programs that you've started.
- **Background Processes**   Shows processes being run in the background by Windows.
- **Windows Processes**   Shows all other processes running on the computer.

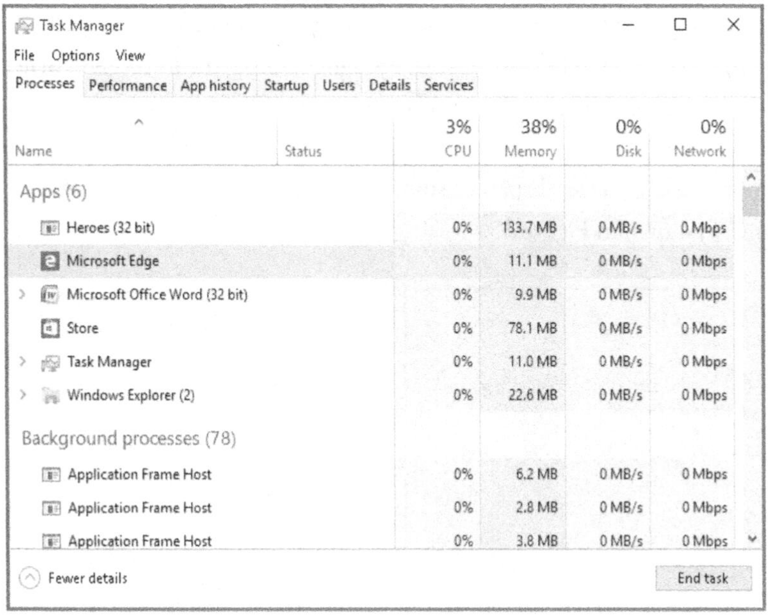

Figure 38 Getting an expanded view of running apps, programs and processes.

Apps, programs and processes are listed by name, status, CPU usage, memory usage, disk usage, and network usage. A blank status indicates a normal state. As with the summary view, you can exit an application or stop a running process by clicking the item in the Task list, and then clicking End Task.

Some items with related windows or processes can be expanded. Double-click an item to see details for the related windows or processes. Display more management options by right-clicking an item in the Task list. The options include:

- **Open File Location**   Opens the folder containing the executable file for the application or process in File Explorer
- **Create Dump File**   Creates a memory dump file for the selected process
- **Go To Details**   Opens the Details tab with the process selected
- **Properties**   Opens the Properties dialog box for the executable file.

Although programs you are running are listed under the Apps heading, programs being run by any other users (such as when you switch context) are listed as Background Processes. Select the Users tab to view information about resources being used by other users.

Folder Options: Quick Reference

Option	Description
Always Show Icons, Never Thumbnails	When selected, does not create thumbnails. Instead, File Explorer shows the standard file and folder icons. Otherwise, shows large thumbnail images of the actual content for pictures and other types of files. When folders have many pictures, showing thumbnails can slow down the display because File Explorer has to create the thumbnail representation of each image.
Always Show Menus	When selected, always shows the menu bar, providing quick access to the menus. (You can also toggle this option by clicking Organize, pointing to Layout, and then selecting Menu Bar.) Otherwise, hides the menu bar; you must elect to display it by pressing the Alt key.
Display File Icon On Thumbnails	When selected, adds file icons to thumbnails it displays. Otherwise, displays thumbnails without file icons.
Display File Size Information In Folder Tips	When selected, displays a tooltip showing the creation date and time, the size of the folder, and a partial list of files when you move the mouse pointer over a folder name or folder icon. Otherwise, displays a tooltip showing the creation date and time when you move the mouse pointer over a folder name or folder icon.

Option	Description
Display The Full Path In The Title Bar	When selected and you press Alt+Tab to access the flip view, displays the actual file path instead of the folder name when you move the mouse pointer over a File Explorer window. Otherwise, when you press Alt+Tab to access the flip view, displays the folder name when you move the mouse pointer over a File Explorer window.
Hidden Files And Folders	When you select the related Show option, displays hidden files, folders, or drives. Otherwise, does not display hidden files, folders, or drives.
Hide Empty Drives	When selected, displays information about empty drives in the This PC window. Otherwise, does not display information about empty drives in the Computer window.
Hide Extensions For Known File Types	When selected, does not display file extensions for known file types. Otherwise, displays file extensions for known file types.
Hide Folder Merge Conflicts	When selected, merge conflicts aren't displayed for folders. Otherwise, displays merge conflicts.

Option	Description
Hide Protected Operating System Files	When selected, does not display operating system files. Otherwise, displays operating system files. Hidden operating system files are also referred to as super hidden files.
Launch Folder Windows In A Separate Process	When selected, runs in a separate process each time it is opened. Otherwise, Windows runs all instances of File Explorer in the same process.
Open Each Folder In The Same Window	When selected, opens subfolders that you access in the same window. Otherwise, opens subfolders that you access in a new window.
Restore Previous Folder Windows At Logon	When selected, reopens folder windows you were using last time you logged on. Otherwise, folder windows aren't reopened.
Show Drive Letters	When selected, displays drive letters as part of the information on the Locations bar. Otherwise, does not display drive letters as part of the information on the Locations bar.

Option	Description
Show Encrypted Or Compressed NTFS Files In Color	When selected, lists encrypted files and compressed files using different colors. Normally, encrypted files are displayed with green text and compressed files are displayed with blue text. Otherwise, does not distinguish among encrypted, compressed, and normal files.
Show Pop-Up Description For Folder And Desktop Items	When selected, shows tooltips with additional information about a file or folder when you move the mouse over the file or folder. Otherwise, does not show tooltips with additional information about a file or folder when you move the mouse over the file or folder.
Show Preview Handlers In Preview Pane	When selected and the Preview pane is visible, displays previews of selected files and folders. Otherwise, when the Preview pane is visible, previews of selected files and folders aren't displayed.
Single-Click To Open An Item	When selected, selects an item when you point to it and opens the item when you click once. Otherwise, selects an item when you click it; opens the item when you double-click it.

Option	Description
Use Check Boxes To Select Items	When selected, displays check boxes that you can use to select files. Otherwise, allows you to select files, folders, and other items using only the standard selection techniques such as click, Shift+Click, and Ctrl+Click.
Use Sharing Wizard	When selected, uses the File Sharing wizard for configuring file sharing. Otherwise, uses the advanced file sharing options.
When Typing Into A List View	When you select Automatically Type... and are working with the list view, text you type is entered into the Search box. Otherwise, when you are working with the list view and press a letter key, the first file or folder with that letter is selected.

About the Author

William R. Stanek (http://www.williamstanek.com/) has more than 20 years of hands-on experience with advanced programming and development. He is a leading technology expert, an award-winning author, and a pretty-darn-good instructional trainer. Over the years, his practical advice has helped millions of programmers, developers, and network engineers all over the world. His current and books include *Windows 8.1 Administration Pocket Consultant*, *Windows Server 2012 R2 Pocket Consultant* and *Windows Server 2012 R2 Inside Out*.

William has been involved in the commercial Internet community since 1991. His core business and technology experience comes from more than 11 years of military service. He has substantial experience in developing server technology, encryption, and Internet solutions. He has written many technical white papers and training courses on a wide variety of topics. He frequently serves as a subject matter expert and consultant.

William has an MS with distinction in information systems and a BS in computer science, magna cum laude. He is proud to have served in the Persian Gulf War as a combat crewmember on an electronic warfare aircraft. He flew on numerous combat missions into Iraq and was awarded nine medals for his wartime service, including one of the United States of America's highest flying honors, the Air Force Distinguished Flying Cross. Currently, he resides in the Pacific Northwest with his wife and children.

William recently rediscovered his love of the great outdoors. When he's not writing, he can be found hiking, biking, backpacking, traveling, or trekking in search of adventure with his family!

Find William on Twitter at www.twitter.com/WilliamStanek and on Facebook at www.facebook.com/William.Stanek.Author.

Windows PowerShell 3.0 and Windows PowerShell 4.0

ᴛʜᴇPERSONAL
TRAINER™

Windows PowerShell

WILLIAM STANEK
Award-winning technology expert

CPSIA information can be obtained at www.ICGtesting.com
Printed in the USA
LVOW03s1535090815

449425LV00007BA/89/P